NEW VANGUARD 350

GERMAN MARDERS OF WORLD WAR II

The Wehrmacht's prime tank destroyers

STEVEN J. ZALOGA ILLUSTRATED BY FELIPE RODRÍGUEZ

OSPREY PUBLISHING
Bloomsbury Publishing Plc
Kemp House, Chawley Park, Cumnor Hill, Oxford OX2 9PH, UK
Bloomsbury Publishing Ireland Limited,
29 Earlsfort Terrace, Dublin 2, D02 AY28, Ireland
1385 Broadway, 5th Floor, New York, NY 10018, USA
E-mail: info@ospreypublishing.com
www.ospreypublishing.com

OSPREY is a trademark of Osprey Publishing Ltd

First published in Great Britain in 2026

A catalog record for this book is available from the British Library.

ISBN: PB 9781472872142; eBook 9781472872159;
ePDF 9781472872135; XML 9781472872302

26 27 28 29 30 10 9 8 7 6 5 4 3 2 1

Index by Richard Munro
Typeset by Lumina Datamatics Ltd
Printed by Repro India Ltd.

Title page caption: see page 15.

Author's Note

Unless otherwise noted, all photographs are from US archives including the US National Archives and Records Administration, US Army Heritage and Education Center, the Ft Knox Patton Museum, and the former Aberdeen Proving Ground Ordnance Museum.

Abt	*Abteilung*, battalion
Aufklärungs	reconnaissance
Ausf	*Ausführung*, variant
BMM	*Böhmisch-Mährische Maschinenfabrik AG*
bodenständig	static, fixed-site
ČKD	*Českomoravská-Kolben-Daněk*
FAMO	*Fahrzeug und Motoren Werke*
Funksprechgerät	radio
gem	*gemischt*, mixed
GenInsPzTp	*Generalinspektion der Panzertruppe*
HPzJgAbt	*Heeres Panzerjager Abteilung*, army tank destroyer battalion
HG	*Heeresgruppe*, Army Group
Hptm	*Hauptmann*, Captain
HWA	*Heereswaffenamt*, Army Ordnance Department
Instandsetzung	repair
KAN	*Kriegsausrüstungsnachweisung*, war equipment allotments
Ko	*Kompanie*, Company
Kradschützen	motorcycle
KStN	*Kriegsstärkenachweisung*, war strength authorization
leFH	*Leichte feldhaubitze*, light field howitzer
LrS	*Lorraine Schlepper*
Marder	European pine marten
mSPW	*mittlerer Schützenpanzerwagen*, medium armored infantry vehicle
obr	*Obrazets*, variant (Russian)
Ostfront	Eastern Front
Pak	*Panzerabwehr Kanone*
Pak Sfl	*Panzer Abwehr Kanone Selbstfahrlafette*, self-propelled antitank gun
Panzerbefehlswagen	armored command vehicle
Panzerjäger	tank hunter
Pz Sfl	*Panzer Selbstfahrlafette*, armored self-propelled mount
Pzgr	*Panzergranate*, antitank projectile
PzKpfw	*Panzerkampfwagen*, tank
RSO	*Raupenschlepper Ost*, tractor for the East
Schnelle	Fast
Schützen	Motor infantry
SdKfz	*Sonderkraftfahrzeug*, special vehicle
StuG	*Sturmgeschutz*, assault gun
Tropen	Tropical
Unteroffizier	Non-commissioned officer
WUMAG	*Waggon und Maschinenbau AG*
Zug	platoon

CONTENTS

GERMAN MARDERS OF WORLD WAR II

The Wehrmacht's prime tank destroyers

INTRODUCTION

The unexpected appearance of the heavily armored Soviet T-34 and KV tanks at the start of Operation *Barbarossa* in June 1941 caused a tank panic in German infantry units. Infantry defenses were overrun on numerous occasions when their 3.7cm antitank guns could not penetrate the armor of the Soviet tanks. This tank panic led to the development of the Marder tank destroyers. These used light tank chassis and were armed with war-booty Soviet F-22 7.62cm or German 7.5cm Pak 40 antitank guns. These became a very important component of the German armored force in the key battles of 1942–43, including Stalingrad and Kursk. The Marder subsequently fell out of favor due to its weak armored protection.

The Marder name for this type of *Panzerjäger* (Tank hunter) was applied late in its production run. Hitler was annoyed by the inconsistent and convoluted names given to various German armored vehicles. In a directive on November 29, 1943, he suggested a variety of more evocative names. The various Panzerjäger armed with the 7.5cm Pak 40 were named as *Marder*, the German name for the European pine marten, a type of weasel. This name was retroactively applied to earlier types, with those on the Lorraine chassis receiving the designation Marder I, on the PzKpfw II chassis the Marder II, and those on the PzKpfw 38(t) chassis, the Marder III. This name change was formally applied by the OKW (*Oberkommando der Wehrmacht*, Armed Forces High Command) on February 1, 1944, and by the OKH (*Oberkommando des Heeres*, Army High Command) on February 27, 1944. This book uses these names for simplicity's sake, even when describing them in prior years before the name was formally applied.

A 7.5cm PaK 40 auf LrS (Marder I) lost in Vesoul on September 12, 1944 during the fighting with the US 36th Infantry Division. The town was being defended by Schnelle-Abt.602 of the 16.Infanterie-Division, but this Marder I may have come from other LXVI.Korps units retreating through the area at the time.

DIVISIONAL ANTITANK DEFENSE

Germany began forming dedicated *Kampfwagenabwehr-Abteilungen* (tank defense battalions) in October 1934 that were eventually assigned to the Panzertruppen. These used three companies of 3.7cm Pak (*Panzerabwehr Kanone*) towed by trucks. They were subsequently renamed as *Panzerabwehr* (tank defense), and finally as *Panzerjäger* (tank hunters) on March 16, 1940.

At the start of World War II, German infantry divisions deployed their towed antitank guns in several formations. The early divisions had a *Panzerabwehr-Abteilung* (battalion) with three companies with nine guns each, for a total of 27 antitank guns. The infantry divisions were created in "waves," the later waves having the battalion reduced to a single company due to equipment shortages. Each infantry regiment was allotted a *Panzerabwehr-Kompanie* (tank defense company), also called the 14.Kompanie. The divisional *Aufklärungs-Abteilung* (reconnaissance battalion) had a single *Zug* (platoon) with three antitank guns. There was some variation in these units, with some motorized and others still using horse traction.

The Panzer division had fewer towed antitank guns, with none in the Panzer regiments, since they already had ample antitank weapons. As in the case of the infantry, the division deployed a Panzerabwehr-Abteilung with three companies with 27 antitank guns. The *Schützenbrigaden* (motor infantry brigades) had two platoons with three guns each. The *Kradschützen-Abteilung* (motorcycle battalion) and Aufklärungs-Abteilung each had a platoon with three guns each. All antitank guns in the Panzer division were motorized.

The first self-propelled Panzerjäger was created by mounting the Czechoslovak 4.7cm antitank gun on the PzKpfw I Ausf B chassis. By May 1940, at the start of the Battle of France, there were 100 in service. These were not intended for divisional defense but rather were assigned at field army level as a mobile tank destroyer force. Four of these Heeres Panzerjäger-Abteilungen were deployed in 1940. The organization differed due to early equipment shortages, with some battalions having three companies with

The three principal German anti-tank guns in 1942–43 were the 7.5cm Pak 40 in the foreground, the 5cm Pak 38 in the center and the 3.7cm Pak in the background.

six Panzerjäger each and the others having the full complement of three companies with nine each.

The France campaign revealed that the 3.7cm Pak was inadequate due to the growing thickness of tank armor. When the war started in 1939, the *Heereswaffenamt* (HWA, Army Ordnance Department) was already developing a more powerful antitank gun, the 5cm Pak 38. This entered production in the spring of 1940, but none were deployed during the campaign in France. At the time of the invasion of the Soviet Union in 1941, there were 1,047 5cm guns on hand. Since this was not sufficient to re-equip all units, the practice in the infantry divisions' Panzerjäger-Abteilungen was to add a fourth Zug to each company, with two 5cm Pak 38s, bringing the battalion to 27 3.7cm Pak and six 5cm Pak 38 guns. However, not all infantry divisions received the new equipment, and those battalions without the new guns sometimes received additional 3.7cm Paks, bringing their total to 36 guns.

The initial infantry reaction to the 5cm Pak 38 was mixed. Although its greater firepower was appreciated, its 1-tonne weight meant that it was very difficult for its crew to move by hand. This was a significant tactical issue, since once deployed, the prime mover used to tow the gun withdrew to a safer location. Once the gun fired, its location was immediately evident to the enemy and hostile fire could be expected. The usual tactical response was for the crew to move the gun by hand to a secondary location. This might be possible in some terrain conditions, but in mud or snow, it was often impossible.

A Marder III Ausf. H of 1.Kompanie, Panzerjäger-Abteilung.171, 71.Infanterie-Division knocked off the road near Esperia, Italy on May 17, 1944 by Allied bombardment during the fighting in the Cassino area. Here it was being inspected by Free French troops of the 3e Division d'Infanterie Algérienne a day later.

The tank crisis of 1941

The unexpected appearance of the Soviet T-34 and KV tanks at the start of Operation *Barbarossa* in June 1941 created tank panic in many German infantry units. Most units were still dependent on the old 3.7cm Pak. Neither the 3.7cm nor 5cm Pak could penetrate the frontal armor of the new Soviet tanks at typical combat ranges. The 3.7cm gun had already been mocked as the *Heeresanklopfgerät* (army door-knocking gun) or *Panzeranklopfkanone* (tank door-knocking gun) after its encounters with heavily armored Allied tanks in France in 1940, such as the French Char B1 bis and British Matilda.

The HWA was aware of the shortcomings of these guns. A variety of solutions were in the works, including better ammunition using a tungsten-carbide core round, the Panzergranate 40. However, tungsten carbide was in short supply and this type of ammunition was handed out sparingly. In the case of the 5cm Pak 38, the usual steel Pzgr 39 could penetrate 61mm of armor at 500m at 30 degrees inclination, while the Pzgr 40 with the tungsten carbide core could penetrate 86mm at the same range.

Rheinmetall-Borsig had already received a contract in 1939 to develop a 7.5cm antitank gun.

This was essentially a scaled-up 5cm Pak 38. Aside from its larger bore diameter, the new 7.5cm Pak 40 used a much larger propellant case containing about three times as much propellant, 2.7kg vs 0.9kg. As a result, its antitank performance was substantially better, even when using conventional steel shot. On the negative side, the growing shortage of light metal alloys due to the demand of the German aircraft industry meant that the 7.5cm Pak 40 was manufactured entirely from steel and so was significantly heavier than the 5cm Pak 38, 1,425kg vs 1,000kg.

Another Marder III Ausf. H Panzerjäger-Abteilung.171, 71.Infanterie-Division knocked out in the town of Aquino during the fighting on May 19, 1944 in the Cassino area.

The gun's heavy weight was one of the main reasons for its slow adoption, since the infantry branch was not happy with such a cumbersome gun. The 7.5cm Pak 40 was intended from the outset for motorized towing, and the prime mover was intended to be a SdKfz 11 1-tonne half-track. In view of the infantry complaints about the weight of the 5cm Pak 38, the 7.5cm Pak 40 was far too heavy for its six-man crew to easily relocate to a new firing position.

The first 7.5cm Pak 40 were delivered in February 1942 but it did not enter widespread use on the *Ostfront* (Eastern Front) until the autumn of 1942. The first recorded combat losses were recorded in November 1942. Curiously enough, the first heavy antitank guns to reach Wehrmacht service were not German, but Soviet guns, as is described below.

The attempts to reinforce antitank defenses in 1942 had spotty results. By mid-1942, infantry Panzerjäger companies ended up with a mixture of equipment, typically consisting of two heavy (*schwere*) Pak, two medium (*mittlere*) Pak, and six light (*leichte*) 3.7cm Pak guns. The heavy Pak guns were a mixed bag, consisting of the 7.5cm Pak 40 as well as improvised types such as the 7.5cm Pak 97/38. This was an expedient antitank gun made by combining the tube from the old French M1897 75mm gun with the carriage of the 5cm Pak 38. In the antitank role, it mainly fired special shaped-charge antitank rounds that gave it a modest antitank capability. The better heavy Pak guns such as the 7.5cm Pak 40 and ex-Soviet 7.62cm Pak 36 were generally reserved for the divisional Panzerjäger-Abteilung, not the regimental companies. The medium guns were mainly the 5cm Pak 38, but there were also some war-booty weapons in use, including Czech and French 4.7cm guns. A new category, very heavy (*sehr schwere*) Pak guns, was in development, but these 8.8cm versions were not available until 1943.

THE SOVIET VIPER

The Wehrmacht captured large quantities of Soviet artillery at the outset of Operation *Barbarossa* in June 1941. The standard Soviet antitank gun, the 45mm obr 1932, was not of much help in solving the tank crisis as it was a license-built copy of the German 3.7cm Pak. The main difference was that

The basis for the 7.62cm Pak 36 was the Soviet 76mm F-22 divisional gun. This is a rare example of the original configuration with the early pattern wheels, preserved for many years at the Ordnance Museum at Aberdeen Proving Ground after having been captured from the Wehrmacht in World War II. (Author)

the tube diameter had been increased to permit it to fire high-explosive ammunition since it was viewed in the Red Army as a dual-purpose infantry gun.

The gun that caught German attention was the 76mm F-22 obr 36. This gun is frequently misidentified as a Soviet antitank gun; it was actually a divisional gun (*divizionaya pushka*) that played the same field artillery role as the German 10.5cm lFH 18, British 25-pdr, or US 105mm howitzer.

The F-22 was so attractive for the antitank role because it had an unusually long barrel for a field gun, and so very good antiarmor penetration. This feature stemmed from the gun's unusual origins. In the early 1930s, the Red Army became fascinated by reports from its intelligence agencies that Western armies were adopting "universal" field guns in the 75mm range that could be used both as field guns and antiaircraft guns. The Vasiliy Grabin design bureau located at the Novoye Sormovo Plant No 92 in Gorkiy responded with their F-22 design. After testing, it was accepted for use in the Red Army in May 1936. A total of 2,844 F-22 guns were manufactured from 1936–39. Although a very powerful weapon, the F-22 was very heavy at 1,620kg, and the "universal" role had proven to be a fantasy since such a gun did not have quick-enough traverse to track enemy aircraft. As a result, in March 1937, the Red Army requested a "classical" divisional gun. Grabin responded with the F-22 USV (Usovershenstvovanniy, improved), implying it was simply an upgraded F-22 gun. In fact, it was an almost completely new design. The barrel was shorter than the original F-22, L/42 vs L/51, so its antitank performance was not as good. But this didn't matter to the Red Army, as it was intended as a divisional gun.

The Wehrmacht captured a large number of F-22 guns in 1941, perhaps as many as 1,300. Some German field artillery units immediately put them into service, since a significant amount of Soviet ammunition had also been captured. The Wehrmacht initially called them the FK 36 (r) (Feldkanone 36), though they later received the *Kennnummer* (identification number) FK 296(r). Captured F-22 USV guns were called the 7.62cm FK 297(r).

Some F-22 guns were delivered to Rheinmetall for technical exploitation. The German engineers concluded that the F-22 could be easily converted into

A

PAK SFL 1 (7.62cm PAK 36)

1. Pak Sfl 1 (7.62cm Pak 36), Panzerjäger-Abteilung 721, Soviet Union, 1942. The Pak Sfl 1 was originally delivered in the standard overall finish of *Dunkelgrau* Nr. 46 (dark grey), later redesignated as RAL 7021. The markings here are simple, the "1" indicated 1.Kompanie, the "5" indicated the 5th vehicle. The battalion insignia was deer antlers. On the side is the usual *Balkenkreuz* in white and black.

2. Pak Sfl 1 (7.62cm Pak 36), SS-Panzerjäger-Ausbildungs-Abteilung.2, Netherlands, 1944. A small number of Pak Sfl 1 survived into 1943 as training vehicles when they were occasionally repainted in the new scheme of RAL 7028 dark yellow, with bands of RAL 6003 olive green and RAL 8017 red brown. No markings are evident on this vehicle.

1

2

The Soviet F-22 divisional gun was converted into the 7.62cm Pak 36 as seen here in the Fort Sill, Oklahoma museum. It can be distinguished by the muzzle brake and modified splinter shield. Behind it a 7.62cm Pak 39(r), converted from the Soviet F-22-USV. (Author)

an excellent antitank gun by boring out the barrel to accept a larger propellant casing, like that used on the 7.5cm Pak 40. At the same time, Rheinmetall recommended other changes, such as the addition of a muzzle brake to compensate for the additional recoil of the more powerful propellant and the reduction of the excessive splinter shield on the gun. This was approved by the HWA, and in October 1941, Hitler released a directive that the converted 7.62cm Pak 36 guns "are to be produced as quickly and as widely as possible and delivered to the front, to be towed by SdKfz 11 Zugkraftfahrzeuge." The first of the converted antitank guns were delivered in March 1942, and a total of 571 of these towed gun conversions were delivered between 1942 and 1944. Some of the F-22 USVs were also converted as the 7.62cm Pak 39(r), but due to their shorter barrel, antitank performance was about 10–15 percent lower. The upgraded F-22 guns were nicknamed the Viper (*Gadyuka*) by Soviet troops due to their hard-hitting firepower.

MECHANIZING THE WAR-BOOTY ANTITANK GUNS

The availability of the converted Soviet guns raised the possibility of creating a powerful new Panzerjäger by combining the F-22 gun with a tank chassis. This had already been done with the Czech 4.7cm antitank gun, mounted on obsolete PzKpfw I and captured French Renault R 35 light tanks. By the end of 1941, it was obvious that light tanks such as the PzKpfw II and PzKpfw 38(t) were obsolete, and these were large enough to mount the Soviet guns.

The first of these was the PzSfl 1 (Panzer Selbstfahrlafette 1 für 7.62cm Pak 36 SdKfz 131), approved on December 20, 1941. These were built on 150 surplus chassis originally earmarked for the PzKpfw II Ausf D2 light tank or PzKpfw II (*Flamm*) flamethrower tank. A thinly armored, open-topped superstructure was built over the existing chassis, with the gun added centrally above. To reduce the burden to the chassis, the gun was protected by a modest splinter shield. Production at the Alkett plant in Berlin-Borsigwalde began in April 1942 and all 150 were completed by May 1942. A second batch was built later in the year using refurbished chassis.

The 7.62cm PzSfl 1 was based on the chassis of the canceled PzKpfw II Ausf. D. As a result, its production run was short with only 180 built.

The new PzSfl 1s were issued mainly to Panzerjäger-Abteilungen in motorized infantry divisions and SS formations, as well as to separate Panzerjäger battalions subordinate to field armies. In the separate battalions, the plan was to equip the Panzerjäger-Abteilung with 12 each, enough for two companies, while the third company in each battalion would retain its 4.7cm Pak(t) Sfl. The Panzerjäger vehicles were not issued to heavy companies in the infantry regiments, only to the divisional antitank battalions.

These vehicles began seeing extensive combat by the summer of 1942, and were appreciated as a major advance over the older tank destroyers using the 4.7cm Pak (t) gun. Units complained that the vehicle was too high and thus difficult to conceal. In addition, many units felt that the 30 rounds of ammunition stowed on the vehicle were not sufficient and the vehicle was too cramped to store much more. There were also many small technical faults with the vehicle and gun. Nevertheless, the gun was quite good. For example, Panzerjäger-Abteilung 611 reported that it had knocked out 18 Soviet tanks for a loss of only one of their PzSfl 1s.

The PzSfl 1 suffered severe attrition through the 1942 fighting and into early 1943. For example, Panzerjäger-Abteilung 611 mentioned above was wiped out in Stalingrad. By the spring of 1943, there were still about 30 in service, though only some ten to 15 operational at any point in time.

Crew drill on a PzSfl 1 Ausf. D2 of Panzerjäger-Abteilung SS-Division "Wiking" in the summer of 1942. This battalion received a dozen of these in the spring of 1942. This image highlights the awkward height of the vehicle.

This is one of the field expedient 5cm Pak 38 auf PzKpfw II by Pz.Ins.Abt.559 for Panzerjäger-Abteilung.128 with a normal Marder II named "Betti" behind it.

The PzSfl 1 was followed almost immediately by a similar conversion on the PzKpfw 38(t) chassis, the PzSfl 2 (Panzer Selbstfahrlafette 2 für 7.62cm Pak 36 SdKfz 139). Approved on December 22, 1941, a contract was awarded to BMM on March 6, 1942. BMM (Böhmisch-Mährische Maschinenfabrik AG) was the German name for the Czech tank plant ČKD (Českomoravská-Kolben-Daněk) that had developed the PzKpfw 38(t) before the war. Hitler had already clearly stated that he thought that the PzKpfw 38(t) was obsolete even as a reconnaissance tank and that Czech production should be entirely shifted to self-propelled guns.

The PzSfl 2 was similar to its twin, with a lightly armored gun mounting on top of a new superstructure. The PzSfl 2 was built in three contract batches. The initial 194 vehicles were based on the PzKpfw 38(t) Ausf G with the TNHP engines, while the final batch were on the PzKpfw 38(t) Ausf H chassis with the Praga AC engines, which offered a performance increase from 120–150hp. During production, a *Tropen* (Tropical) variation was developed based on the need for better tank destroyers in North Africa. This included new dust filters for the engine, improved air flow for engine and crew cooling, and many other small changes. A total of 57 PzSfl 2s were built in the *Tropen* configuration. An undetermined number of additional PzSfl2s were completed without formal contracts when damaged PzKpfw 38(t) tanks were sent back to BMM for rebuilding.

In contrast to the PzSfl 1, the PzSfl 2 was issued primarily to the Panzerjäger-Abteilungen of Panzer divisions. Panzerarmee Afrika was allotted 36 of the *Tropen* version. The firepower of the PzSfl 2 was appreciated, though ammunition stowage was viewed as too small in number and too awkward to easily access in combat. Initial operational reports from the Ostfront noted the usual sorts of technical problems. An almost universal complaint was the weakness of the forward travel lock. Many of the problems were related to the overworked PzKpfw 38(t) chassis, such as poor floatation due to its narrow tracks, and slow speed due to the added weight of the gun and superstructure. As was the case with the PzSfl 1, the PzSfl 2 had inadequate armored protection for the gun crew, particularly in circumstances when

B

PAK SFL 2 (7.62cm PAK 36)

1. Pak Sfl 2 (7.62cm Pak 36), Panzerjäger-Abteilung.140, 22.Panzer-Division, Kerch Peninsula, Soviet Union, Summer 1942. The Pak Sfl 2 were delivered in the standard *Dunkelgrau* (dark grey) RAL 7021. This unit used simple playing card symbols, seen here beneath the vehicle name Marlies. The *Balkenkreuz* was obscured when given an impromptu camouflage of mud.

2. Pak Sfl 2 (7.62cm Pak 36), 2./Panzerjäger-Abteilung.61, 11.Panzer-Division, southern France, August 1944. Older Pak Sfl 2 such as this one originally finished in overall *Dunkelgrau* were often refinished in the 1943/44 scheme of RAL 7028 dark yellow when returned to the factory for rebuilding. After being issued to their units, they were then camouflaged by the unit with airbrushed bands of RAL 6003 olive green and RAL 8017 red brown.

1

2

A PzSfl 2 für 7.62cm Pak 36 captured by Allied forces in Tunisia in 1943. These were from the *Tropen* series with air filters and other modifications for desert operation.

it was employed against doctrine without sufficient friendly infantry cover. By the time of the offensive near Kursk in the summer of 1943, barely a third of the vehicles were still operational due to combat attrition.

One of the main reasons for the end of production of the PzSfl 2 was the exhaustion of the supply of captured Soviet F-22 guns. A total of 571 towed guns were modernized as the 7.62cm Pak 36, while about 530 guns were used for the Panzerjäger conversions for a grand total of about 1,100 guns. An additional number of guns were used by German field artillery units in the original 7.62cm FK 36 (r) configuration. The later F-22-USV gun was not used for Panzerjäger conversions because it had inadequate antitank performance.

Production of Panzerjäger with 7.62cm Pak 36

Type	**PzSfl 1**	**PzSfl 2**
Chassis	**PzKpfw II**	**PzKpfw 38(t)**
1942		
Apr	60	68
May	90	52
Jun		23
Jul		50
Aug		51
Sep	15	50
Oct	7	50
1943		
May	4	
Jun	4	
Total	**180**	**344**

The PzSfl 2 für 7.62cm Pak 36 was not widely used in France in 1944 except with Panzerjäger-Abteilung.61 of the 11.Panzer-Division in southern France. This example from 3.Kompanie was lost in the Montélimard region during the August 1944 fighting.

Mechanizing the 7.5cm Pak 40 antitank gun

A detail view of the fighting compartment of the PzSfl 2 für 7.62cm Pak 36 preserved for many years at the Ordnance Museum at Aberdeen Proving Ground. (Author)

The limited availability of the war-booty Soviet guns meant that the production of Panzerjäger would have to be switched to the new 7.5cm Pak 40 gun. The first of these types were based on the war-booty French Lorraine tractor and the obsolete PzKpfw II chassis.

In early 1942, Hitler was shown a conversion developed by the Baukommando Becker consisting of a French Chenilette Lorraine 37L converted into a *Geschützwagen* (gun vehicle) fitted with the 10.5cm leFH 18 field howitzer in an armored box at the rear of the chassis. As a result, Hitler told *Reichsminister für Bewaffnung und Munition* (Minister for Weapons and Munitions) Albert Speer that all available Lorraine tractors should be converted into self-propelled guns. Hauptmann Albert Becker was an artillery officer whose family ran a construction business. Using his family's resources, from 1940–41 he converted some war booty British Mk VI light tanks into self-propelled howitzers to mechanize his towed artillery battery. The success of this venture was brought to Hitler's attention. With Hitler's approval, in 1941 Hptm Becker was authorized to create a small engineering consortium linking the Alkett plant near Berlin with Becker's metalworking plant in Krefeld and the Hotchkiss plant in Saint-Denis, outside of Paris. This eventually was designated as Bauart Panzerkampfwagen-Instandsetzung-Abteilung Paris (*bodenständig*).

In May 1942, Alkett used Becker's plans to design an armored superstructure and associated equipment to mount the 7.5cm Pak 40 on the Lorraine chassis. This design was approved and Alkett manufactured the armored subassembly at their Berlin-Borsigwalde plant. Final assembly of the Panzerjäger LrS (*Lorraine Schlepper*) für 7.5cm Pak 40/1 SdKfz 135 was assigned to the Hotchkiss plant in Paris and HKB Bielitz at Bielsko-Biała in occupied Poland. This vehicle was later designated as the Marder I.

An emergency deployment of six Panzerjäger companies to infantry divisions of *Heeresgruppe Mitte* (Army Group Center) on the Eastern Front began in August 1942. Despite concerns that the Lorraine tractor would not prove durable enough, the value of the new 7.5cm Pak 40 gun convinced the divisions to make careful use

A Marder I 7.5cm Pak 40/1 auf Geschützwagen Lorraine Schlepper (f) of 1.Kompanie, Panzerjäger-Abteilung.15, 15.Infanterie-Division during training in southern France in 1942. The divisional insignia is a silhouette of the Frankfurter Römer, a medieval landmark in the city's old town district.

A Marder I 7.5cm Pak 40/1 auf Geschützwagen Lorraine Schlepper (f) named *Löwe* (Lion) seen here in a US Army holding area south of Trévières in Normandy in the late summer of 1944, probably from either the 709. or 716. Infanterie-Division.

of their new tank destroyers. The Lorraine tank destroyers proved to be adequate in the summer months, but were increasingly unsuitable for use in the autumn rainy season and in snowy winter months due to their narrow tracks and inadequate engines. Nevertheless, these six Panzerjäger companies kept their vehicles in service well into 1943.

Nine of the PzJgLrS 7.5cm Sfls were allotted to Schnelle-Abteilung 334 of the 334.Infantrierie-Division that was dispatched to Tunisia starting in December 1942, where they saw extensive combat use. The majority of the PzJgLrS 7.5cm Sfls were kept in France due to concern by the HWA over the vehicle's durability. These were used in Panzerjager-Abteilungen of various infantry divisions while in training in France, usually equipping one company in each battalion. At the time of the D-Day invasion in June 1944, there were about a hundred of these in service in France, including companies with the 709. and 716. Infanterie-Divisionen that defended the invasion beaches. A handful survived in Alsace in January 1945 with the 245. and 719.Infanterie-Divisionen.

Once the supply of Lorraine tractors was exhausted, Becker turned his attention to other chassis. Ten FCM 36 infantry tanks were modified with the 7.5cm Pak 40, as well as 24 Hotchkiss H 38/39 infantry tanks. All of these served with the 21.Panzer-Division in Normandy. Baukommando Becker converted French half-tracks, intended as substitutes for the SdKfz 250 and SdKfz 251 armored half-tracks. The most elaborate of these conversions was the 7.5cm Pak 40 auf mSPW S307(f) that consisted of the 7.5cm Pak 40 antitank gun mounted on a Somua MCG half-track. A total of 72 of these were planned but only 16 were converted. They were used by the Panzergrenadier regiments of the 21.Panzer-Division in Normandy.

The prototype of the 7.5cm Pak Sfl. auf FCM, one of ten completed by the Becker Baukommando at the Hotchkiss plant in the St. Denis suburb of Paris. These served with the 21.Panzer-Division in Normandy in 1942–43 for training.

MARDER II

An overhead view of the 7.5cm Pak Sfl. auf FCM. These seem to have been retired from service in 1943 prior to the summer 1944 campaign in Normandy.

The small number of Lorraine tractors inevitably meant that other chassis would be needed to mechanize the 7.5cm Pak 40. The first of these used the PzKpfw II chassis, initially called the Panzerjäger II für 7.5cm Pak 40/2 (SdKfz 131), and eventually Marder II. The effort began on May 18, 1942, with Rheinmetall-Borsig assigned to modify the gun, Alkett to design the new superstructure, and MAN to adapt the tank chassis. The PzKpfw II Ausf F was produced at FAMO-Ursus from March 1941. This plant in occupied Poland was originally called Ursus, then the *Państwowe Zakłady Inżynieryjne* (National Engineering Works) in the 1930s, when it was nationalized for the production of Polish armored vehicles. It was put under FAMO's control after Poland's defeat in the 1939 campaign and was also sometimes called FAMO-*Warschau* (Warsaw).

The Marder II was a very simple conversion and the prototype entered trials at Alkett in mid-June 1942, barely a month after the start of the design. In contrast to the earlier Panzerjäger armed with the Soviet F-22 gun, the Marder II had the gun mounted in a fixed superstructure with limited traverse. This offered better protection for the crew. The enlarged fighting compartment also permitted better ammunition stowage for 37 rounds, compared to 30 rounds for the previous types. This had been a longstanding complaint about the early Panzerjäger.

The heavy losses of armored vehicles in the Soviet Union in 1941 led Hitler to authorize a new program to increase production, generally dubbed the Adolf Hitler Panzer Program. The second phase, called Program II, began in April 1942. As part of this scheme, in June 1942, Speer discussed the issue of what proportion of the PzKpfw II production would be earmarked for the Marder II. On June 4, Hitler permitted half, but later in the month authorized 75 percent and up to 100 percent if the German Army wanted more.

The prototype of the Marder II in the Alkett factory yard in Berlin-Borsigwalde. It was apparently finished in the *Tropen* scheme, a camouflage pattern developed for the North African theater.

The scale of production at FAMO-Ursus shifted through time due to two related issues. The BMM plant had been assigned a similar Panzerjäger für Pak 40 as described below, so there was an attempt made to balance the two production programs. The PzKpfw II Ausf F tank remained in production by FAMO. In addition, the HWA had developed a self-propelled 10.5cm leFH 18 field gun on the PzKpfw II that entered production in February 1943, later called the Wespe. There was thus continuing debate over the utilization of

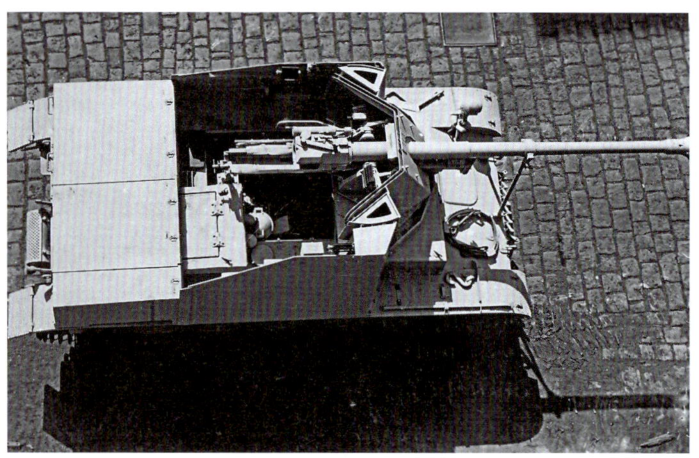

A Marder II from a production batch after December 1942 at the Alkett plant in Berlin-Borsigwalde.

the PzKpfw II chassis. Program III of the Hitler Panzer Program expected FAMO-Ursus to reach a monthly production rate of 55 by May 1943 and 80 by October 1943. However, this plan was abandoned. The Marder II remained in production at FAMO-Ursus only until June 1943, when it was decided to shift production of the plant entirely to the Wespe self-propelled gun.

About 75 Marder IIs were converted between January 1943 and March 1944 by MAN and Škoda, using older PzKpfw II tanks that had been returned to the plants for rebuilding. There were also field conversions of PzKpfw II tanks by the Panzer-Instandsetzung-Abteilung 559 (Tank repair battalion) in Smolensk, Russia. Total new production and conversion totaled about 680 vehicles, far short of the 1,210 new production vehicles intended under the Hitler Panzer Program.

The Marder II was first deployed in September 1942 with the 13.Panzer-Division. Subsequent shipments to the Ostfront went to other Panzer divisions, as well as to infantry divisions, and in separate Panzerjäger companies and battalions assigned to various corps. In June 1943, there were only three of these Panzerjäger Abteilungen on the entire Ostfront.

The troop reactions to the Marder II were generally more favorable than to the two earlier Panzerjäger with the Soviet F-22 guns. The crews found the vehicle stability to be good, although the recoil was severe and loosened many parts. The gun performance was excellent against typical targets such as the T-34 and Lend-Lease types such as the M3 medium tank. The ammunition load of 37 rounds was still inadequate, and crews compensated for this by stowing additional boxes of ammunition on the rear deck, bringing the total to about 60 rounds. The rate of fire was about five rounds per minute, limited mainly by the heavy fumes from the gun.

The armor of the Marder II was inadequate, but it was hoped that proper tactics could mitigate this shortcoming. However, infantry commanders

MARDER I

1. Panzerjäger FCM für 7.5cm Pak 40/1, StuG.Abt.200, 21.Panzer-Division, summer 1943. Ten of these Panzerjäger FCM were built by Baukommando Becker and they served with the 21.Panzer-Division in Normandy. They were finished in the usual 1943–44 scheme of RAL 7028 dark yellow, with bands of RAL 6003 olive green and RAL 8017 red brown. They seem to have been retired before the summer of 1944 as they do not show up on strength reports at the time of the Normandy fighting.

2. Panzerjäger 38H für 7.5cm Pak 40/1, 1./StuG.Abt.200, 21.Panzer-Division, Normandy, July 1944. StuG.Abt.200 was equipped with self-propelled guns built on war-booty French Hotchkiss H 39 light tanks by Baukommando Becker. There were 17 Panzerjäger 38H 7.5cm Pak 40 like the one here and 24 Geschützwagen 10.5cm lFH.18. In July 1944, they were divided up into five companies, consisting of four Pak 40 Panzerjäger and six 10.5cm lFH 18 assault guns. They were finished in the usual 1943–44 scheme of RAL 7028 dark yellow, with bands of RAL 6003 olive green and RAL 8017 red brown. The unit insignia, based on the usual German map symbols, is evident on the front of the superstructure.

1

2

were seldom aware of the limitations of the Panzerjäger and often tried to use them like a normal Panzer or Sturmgeschütz that had much better armor. The Panzerjäger were often instructed to reinforce infantry in close-range support missions. However, their thin armor was vulnerable to common Soviet weapons such as the ubiquitous antitank rifle, and their open tops were exposed to mortar fire.

A pair of Marder II of Panzerjäger-Abteilung Großdeutschland, Panzergrenadier-Division Großdeutschland in Ukraine in the winter of 1943. The battalion received its Marder II in June 1943.

On paper, the Panzerjäger company was authorized an armored munitions carrier, but these were not available so unarmored trucks were used instead. This created a tactical problem, as the trucks couldn't easily move up to the firing positions and often the Panzerjäger had to withdraw to the rear to reload ammunition. Another vehicle that was authorized but seldom available was a PzKpfw I for Panzerjäger battalion commanders.

Ersatz Marder

The shortage of Marders in 1943 led to several attempts at field-expedients substitutes, and at least three examples are known. Panzer-Instandsetzung-Abteilung 559 in Smolensk converted a number of PzKpfw II tanks into Marder IIs (7.5cm) using kits. When these ran out, they made local versions using available materials that differed in the shape of the superstructure. At least one was built using a 5cm Pak 38. Three of these non-standard conversions were supplied to Panzerjäger-Abteilung 128 of the 23.Panzer-Division while it was being rehabilitated in the spring of 1943. The single Marder II (5cm) still appeared on divisional strength reports as late as November 1943 but disappeared on subsequent reports, suggesting it was lost in combat. Panzerjäger-Abteilung 31 of the 31.Infanterie-Division had an improvised 7.5cm Pak 40 on a PzKpfw III chassis at the time of the fighting around Kursk in July 1943.

A Marder II of an unidentified unit in the Soviet Union in the winter of 1943. Crews frequently carried additional boxes of ammunition on the rear deck as seen here due to the limited ammunition stowage of the vehicle.

A more unusual conversion was constructed for Heeres-Panzerjäger-Abteilung 563, serving under 18.Armee of Heeresgruppe Nord in early 1943. This consisted of a captured Soviet T-26 chassis with the turret removed and replaced with the 7.5cm Pak 97/38. Ten of these conversions were completed in July 1943, when they equipped the 4.Kompanie, HPzJgAbt 563. The Red Army's 249th (Estonian)

While this may seem to be an ordinary Marder II, it was one of the 7.5cm Pak 40 field conversions by Pz.Ins.Abt.559 for Panzerjäger-Abteilung.128 of the 23.Panzer-Division as can be seen from the details of the front superstructure.

Rifle Division encountered at least one of these as late as November 1944 during the fighting for Tehumardi, on the island of Saaremaa in the Baltic Sea off the Estonian coast. Other improvised conversions were probably built elsewhere on the Ostfront, but these three examples have been preserved in the surviving records.

MARDER III AUSF H

In May 1943, in parallel with the Marder II program, Hitler approved Speer's plan to switch PzKpfw 38(t) production to a Panzerjäger as part of Program II of the Adolf Hitler Panzer Program. Production of the PzSfl 2 PzKpfw 38(t) was already underway, but the supply of war-booty Soviet 7.62cm Pak 36 guns was evaporating. As a result, BMM was instructed to develop a Panzerjäger using the 7.5cm gun. In March 1942, a program began to adapt the StuG 40 7.5cm gun to the PzKpfw 38(t) chassis. Although a prototype was completed, the program was abandoned in favor of using the more powerful 7.5cm Pak 40 antitank gun, under the codename Siegmar.

The first prototype underwent test firing at the Milowitz (Milovice) proving ground in late June 1942. The layout followed the general pattern of the Marder II rather than the PzSfl 2, with a fixed rather than rotating superstructure. The gun was mounted in a traversing mantlet. Unlike the Marder II, the superstructure of the Marder III offered the gun crew some light overhead armor protection. Production of the 7.5cm Pak 40/3 auf PzKpfw 38(t) Ausf H began in November

The 7.5cm StuK auf PzKpfw 38(t) was a short-lived effort to develop a Panzerjäger using the gun from the StuG III assault gun. It lost to similar designs mounting the 7.5cm Pak 40.

A newly manufactured 7.5cm Pak 40/3 auf Sfl.38 Ausf. H in the yards at the BMM plant.

1942 as the supply of Soviet F-22 guns was exhausted. Besides the production of new vehicles at BMM, a conversion program was started at the old Czechoslovak vehicle repair shop, Autozbrojovka č.1 in Přelouč in Czech Bohemia, that had been renamed as Heeres Kraftfahrzeug Werkstatt Pschelautsch when taken over by BMM. A total of 176 older PzKpfw 38(t) tanks were converted to Panzerjäger at that location.

The experience of the 6.Panzer-Division on the Ostfront with the new vehicle was fairly typical:

> "The Sfl. Pak 40 can only be viewed as an imperfect though useable expedient. Due to its mobility and armor, it is clearly superior to the towed Pak 40. However, it doesn't meet the tactical demands it encounters when facing Russian tanks. The disadvantages for the Sfl. are its high superstructure, weak armor, poor cross-country mobility, and timidity to operate close to enemy tanks due to the risk of being destroyed... A weapon is needed with sufficiently thick armor to 'hunt' an opponent. The Sfl. doesn't possess the needed characteristics, therefore, it can't really be called a tank hunter weapon. Within the arsenal of anti-tank weapons such as the Sturmgeschütz or PzKpfw IV with the long 7.5cm gun, the Sfl. can only play a subordinate role, especially during offensive missions."

This evaluation noted that in recent combat, a Marder III battalion with 18 vehicles knocked out 45 Soviet tanks while losing ten of its own vehicles, whereas a neighboring StuG III battalion with 21 vehicles knocked out 114 while losing only a single one of its own vehicles.

A Marder III Ausf. H that was captured by the US Army in Tunisia and put on display at Aberdeen Proving Ground in 1946. The markings are for Aufklärungs-Abteilung 33, 15.Panzer-Division, apparently due to the substitution of Marder III for mortars in this reconnaissance unit.

Marder 7.5cm Pak 40 Sfl production	Marder I	Marder II	Marder IIIH	Marder IIIM
1942				
June	104	1		
July	66	18		
August		50		
Sept		55		
Oct		59		
Nov		62	42	
Dec		83	68	
1943				
Jan		90	60	
Feb		60	35	
March		11	30	
April		12	34	
May		60	24	20
June		45	60	45
July		12	28	90
August		3	27	62
Sept		22	34	101
Oct		13	8	141
Nov				100
Dec		5		75
1944				
Jan		1		67
Feb				72
March				64
April				59
May				46
Total	**170**	**662**	**450**	**942**

MARDER III AUSF M

The hasty conversion of tank chassis into self-propelled guns inevitably resulted in vehicles that were needlessly high, making them difficult to conceal in battlefield conditions. In addition, mounting the gun and armored superstructure over the middle of the vehicle led to poor weight distribution, which contributed to premature mechanical breakdown. Furthermore, the Adolf Hitler Panzer Program wanted to boost monthly production at BMM to 180 Panzerjäger by September 1943.

To respond to these issues, in early 1943, engineers at BMM and Alkett proposed a significant redesign of the Marder III, both simplifying it to increase production and improving the overall layout. The engine was shifted from the usual rear location to the center of the hull, so the vehicle was codenamed Siegmar M (M = *Mitte*, center). This permitted the fighting compartment to be relocated to a lower position in the rear of the hull. The redesign reduced overall vehicle weight from 10.8 to 10.5 tonnes, even though the superstructure

A newly manufactured 7.5cm Marder III Ausf. M in the yards at the BMM plant.

A 7.5cm Marder III Ausf. M, probably from Panzerjäger-Abteilung 194, 94. Infanterie-Division, captured by the US 85th Infantry Division near Castellonorato on May 16, 1944 during the Cassino fighting.

frontal armor was increased from 15mm to 30mm. As importantly, it reduced vehicle height and placed the gun crew in a more sheltered position behind the engine. Other changes were introduced to speed production, including the greater use of welding instead of bolted construction. A prototype was constructed at BMM from January–February 1943. Series production began in May 1943. The third phase of the Adolf Hitler Panzer Program envisioned manufacturing 950 Marder IIs between May 1943 and March 1944, and this objective was actually exceeded.

Due to its extensive production run, the Marder III Ausf M had numerous production changes. In July 1943, the Ausf IV 180hp turbocharged engine was introduced, but it had to be replaced by the less powerful Type NS 160hp engine in November 1943 because the Ausf IV engine tended to blow out head gaskets. The engine exhaust was changed in July 1943, with the exhaust pipe routed outside the right side of the hull before connecting to the muffler at the rear. Due to complaints about the poor radios used in previous Panzerjäger, a specialized Befehlsjäger command vehicle was introduced that was fitted with both a long-range Fu 8 and short-range FuSprGerF radio. The Befehlsjäger 38 Ausf M was usually issued on a scale of one per company for use by the company commander.

The Marder III Ausf M was successful enough that a number of sub-variants were examined. The most important of these were the 15cm SiG 33/1 Grille heavy assault gun and 2cm Flakpanzer 38(t), which both shared the new middle-engine configuration. A test vehicle was manufactured with two gas cylinders to substitute liquified natural gas for gasoline in training units due to widespread fuel shortages. Another experimental prototype removed the gun and plated over the front embrasure. The intention was to use the resulting vehicle as the basis for a family of vehicles, including an ammunition carrier, armored infantry carrier, and mortar carrier. These did not reach series production, as there were other plans for the BMM plant.

The production of the Marder III Ausf M ended in May 1944 due to the transition to production of the Jagdpanzer 38 at BMM. This vehicle, popularly called the Hetzer, was a response to the complaints about the Panzerjäger, as well as the perennial shortage of Sturmgeschütz in the infantry divisions. This is described in more detail below.

This provides details of the 5cm Pak 38 mounting in the improvised Panzerjäger built by Pz.Ins.Abt.559 for Panzerjäger-Abteilung.128 of the 23.Panzer-Division on a PzKpfw II chassis.

Marder deliveries May 1943–September 1944		
	Marder II	**Marder III**
1943		
May	47	35
Jun	68	46
Jul		134
Aug	15	63
Sep		104
Oct	13	115
Nov	9	118
Dec	9	87
1944		
Jan	8	64
Feb	10	65
Mar		96
Apr	4	49
May		80
Jun	4	15
Jul		30
Aug		18
Sep		10
Total	**187**	**1,129**

MARDER SUBSTITUTE: THE RSO

There were never enough Panzerjäger to provide all infantry divisions with a self-propelled company. Furthermore, there were increasing complaints about the difficulty of using the towed 7.5cm Pak 40. To supplement production of the Marder series, Rheinmetall proposed mounting the Pak 40 on top of the Steyr Raupenschlepper Ost (RSO) prime mover. The RSO was a fully tracked prime mover used as a substitute for the SdKfz 11 1-tonne half-track, especially on the Ostfront. It entered use in infantry divisions in 1942, some being used for towing the Pak 40.

A prototype 7.5cm Pak 40 auf RSO was built in July 1943 by Steyr. The driving compartment was completely redesigned to permit 360-degree gun traverse, and the cab was lightly armored. Initial firing trials proved the basic concept. The initial scheme was to have the Pak 40/4 gun carried on one RSO, while a second RSO would carry a jib crane and a normal gun carriage to permit the gun to be dismounted from the first RSO and used as a towed gun.

Hitler approved the concept in early August 1943. In September 1943, Gen. Wolfgang Thomale, the chief-of-staff of the General Inspectorate of the Panzer Forces, recommended limited production to permit operational combat trials as soon as possible on the Ostfront. Hitler was shown a prototype in October 1943, and after the pre-production test batch of 50 vehicles he

MARDER ATTACK AT KURSK, JULY 1943

A pair of Marder III Ausf. H (7.5cm Pak 40) of Panzerjäger-Abteilung.10, 10.Panzergrenadier-Division take part in the fighting around Ponyri Station on July 14, 1943 during the battle of Kursk. At the time, the battalion had three companies of the Marder III, numbering 39 vehicles. The battalion took heavy losses during the fighting in the Orel sector and a month later had been reduced to 25 Marder III of which eight were in repair.

122

A 7.5cm Marder Ausf. M of Stabs Kompanie, SS-Panzerjager-Abteilung.16, 16.SS-Panzergrenadier-Division RFSS in November 1944. This Marder took cover in a tunnel in Vado di Monzuna south of Bologna to shell targets in the valley below.

suggested that as many as 400 per month be built if successful.

The trials batch of the basic 7.5cm Pak 40/4 auf RSO was ready later in October 1943, but the design of a crane for the support RSO was not yet completed. As a result, the plan changed to simply releasing the trials vehicles to Heeresgruppe Mitte. Of the 50 initial vehicles, 28 went to Panzerjäger-Abteilung 743, 12 to the Ski-Jäger-Brigade, and the remaining ten served as an army group reserve. The vehicles went into combat in January and February 1944. The results of the combat trials were the subject of a March 1944 report. Although this report praised the added mobility of the gun compared to a towed version, the crew was completely exposed and suffered heavy casualties. When used from stationary entrenchments to reduce crew casualties, the guns were lost when the vehicles suffered combat damage or had mechanical breakdowns. The report recommended the use of more armor protection, a more robust chassis, and facilities to dismount the gun on to a towed carriage, as had originally been planned. Although Hitler gave permission in May 1944 to begin serial production, he reconsidered. On June 4, 1944, the OKH notified Steyr that further production was canceled since the troop trials had revealed the Pak 40 auf RSO to have been a complete failure. Besides the 50 vehicles sent to HG Mitte, a further ten had been produced.

Although production had been cancelled, the Pak 40 auf RSO remained in combat service on the Ostfront after the surviving vehicles were transferred to Heeresgruppe Nord in northern Russia. They served with the Panzerzerstörer-Bataillone 477 and 478 under 18. Armee command, and in Panzerjäger-Abteilungen 263, 751, and 752. Due to heavy attrition in the summer battles, only a handful were still in use in September 1944, after which they largely disappeared. A few survived in Germany and at least one was captured by the US Army in 1945.

Post-Stalingrad Panzerjäger organization

Although a handful of select infantry units, including Waffen-SS formations, received the new Marder Pak Sfl in 1942, the early Pak Sfl were mostly distributed to Panzer divisions, select motorized infantry divisions, and the Heeres-Panzerjäger-Abteilungen. The Marder Pak Sfl was very rare in infantry divisions in 1942.

In contrast to the infantry divisions, the Panzer divisions in 1942 usually had more priority for the supply of new Marders in their Panzerjäger Abteilungen. Under the original KStN 1148a (*Kriegsstärkenachweisung*, Authorized war organization), a Panzerjäger Kompanie had nine PzSfl tank destroyers, with three in each Zug.

Fighting north of St. Mère-Église on D-Day, June 6, 1944 pitted this 7.5cm Panzerjäger 38(t) Ausf. M Marder III, from 1./ Panzerjäger Abt.243 supporting the 91.Luftlande-Division against M4 tanks of Co. C, 746th Tank Battalion supporting the 82nd Airborne Division. This is the scene a few days later after one of the knocked out M4 tanks was pushed off the road to clear it for traffic.

Due to increased production, a modification to this basic organization was made under KStN1148a Behelf (substitute) on December 1, 1942. This raised the standard company strength to ten in divisional companies by giving the company commander a Marder. The separate Heeres Panzerjäger Abteilungen were also reinforced to 13 PzSfls in each company by increasing the Zug strength from three to four and giving the company commander a Marder. This organization change was accompanied by KAN 1148d (*Kriegsausrüstungsnachweisung*, War equipment allotment) that authorized the new Fu 8 Se 30 radio for the company commander and the Funksprechgerat F in each Marder.

There was a trend through early 1943 to increase the number of self-propelled companies in the Panzerjäger Abteilungen of the Panzer divisions from one to two as resources permitted, with the third still using towed 7.5cm Pak 40 guns. In January 1943, the 4.Panzer-Division was the first to have all three companies equipped with Marders. Increased Marder production also permitted company strength to be increased to 14, with four Marders in each of the three Züge and two Marders in the *Stab* (headquarters). This was authorized under KStN 1148d on June 1, 1943. A minor change, also authorized that day under KStN 1155d, allotted three *Panzerbefehlswagen* (armored command vehicles) per Abteilung. This codified the previous efforts to give each company commander a modified Marder with more complete radio equipment.

As the Marder began to equip all the companies in the Panzer divisions' tank destroyer battalion, this organization was increasingly called *Schnelle Panzerjäger Abteilung* to distinguish it from the older towed or hybrid towed/self-propelled battalions. When the new Panzer-Division Type 43 organization was authorized on September 24, 1943, it included the Schnelle Panzerjäger Abteilung.

It should be emphasized that these organizational changes did not mean that all German Panzer divisions actually implemented them. Many units remained at lower strength and in older configurations due to continuing

A pair of 7.5cm Marder III Ausf. M, from 1./Panzerjäger Abt.243, destroyed next to Église Saint-Côme et Saint-Damien on the main road through Roncey in late July 1944 during Operation *Cobra* in Normandy.

shortages of vehicles and equipment. The new KStN organizations were authorized strength, not necessarily actual strength.

A major complaint in Panzerjäger units was the use of the Funksprechgerät D radio, which had an effective range of only about 1–2km. This was a problem, since a Panzerjäger company was typically deployed along a frontline of about 4km. Not only did the radio set lack range, but it was very susceptible to damage from gun recoil. As a result, on November 1, 1943, KAN 1155d authorized substitution of the radio for the Funksprechgerät F.

In spite of increased production of the new 7.5cm Pak 40 and the Pak Sfl, German antitank defenses in early 1943 were still stretched thin due to heavy combat attrition. A survey of all infantry divisions on the Ostfront in April 1943 found that on average, each had 45 antitank guns. Of these, 24 were 3.7cm Pak, ten were 5cm Pak 38, and 11 were heavy antitank guns split between the 7.5cm Pak 40 and 7.5cm Pak 97/38. At the time, there were about 800 7.5cm Pak 40 and 770 Pak 97/38 guns in service. Actual strength from division to division varied widely, not only because of different organizational schemes, but also due to the usual vagaries of combat attrition and spotty resupply.

E

MARDER III AUSF. H

1. Marder III Ausf. H, 1./Panzerjäger-Abteilung.171, 71.Infanterie-Division, Cassino area, Italy, May 1944. This Marder III Ausf. H was painted in a base coat of RAL 7028 dark yellow, with hand-applied camouflage of RAL 6003 olive green and RAL 8017 red brown. On the left side of the superstructure front is the *Kleeblatt* (clover leaf) insignia of the 71.Infanterie-Divison while near it is the white tactical map symbol for a Panzerjäger company.

2. Marder III Ausf. H, Panzerjäger-Abteilung, Heeresgruppe Mitte, Lvov, July 1944. This Marder III Ausf. H was painted in a base coat of RAL 7021 dark grey with an irregular pattern of RAL 7028 dark yellow applied over it. The vehicle tactical number follows the February 16 OKH directive regarding the placement of markings, and it has been applied in a simplified fashion with only the outer white trim.

1
2
332

Marder strength on Ostfront, 1943										
	20 Apr	**10 May**	**31 May**	**30 Jun**	**31 Jul**	**31 Aug**	**30 Sep**	**31 Oct**	**30 Nov**	**31 Dec**
Marder II 7.62cm	16	15	15	25	12	10	9	27	12	11
Marder III 7.62cm	93	99	97	78	92	89	64	46	49	38
Marder I 7.5cm	42	41	41	41	40	35	29	41	40	37
Marder II 7.5cm	279	280	288	335	318	298	253	227	202	196
Marder III 7.5cm	139	149	151	160	176	248	273	427	378	408
Total	**569**	**584**	**592**	**639**	**638**	**680**	**628**	**768**	**681**	**690**

Source: Pak-Lage-Ost (Sf), Gen Qu GenInsPzTp, Jan 1944

A typical example from June 1943 was the 17.Armee serving under Heeresgruppe Nord on the Leningrad Front. It had 30 infantry divisions under its command and only 260 heavy antitank guns, comprising 43 self-propelled and 217 towed guns. Of these, 36 of the towed antitank guns were the powerful 8.8cm Pak 43/41, while the rest were an assortment of 7.5cm Pak 40 and 7.62cm Pak 36 guns. Most of the self-propelled guns were in Heeres-Panzerjäger-Abteilung 563, and there were only eight Marders in infantry division antitank companies. Due to the shortage of Marders in the infantry divisions, it was the usual practice to disperse Heeres-Panzerjäger-Abteilung 563, with each of its four companies going to different infantry divisions.

Marder readiness on Ostfront, December 1, 1943			
Army Group	**Operational**	**Repair**	**Total**
HG Nord	30	1	**31**
HG Mitte	247	134	**381**
HG Süd	211	217	**428**
HG A	32	21	**53**
Total	**520**	**373**	**893**

Source: *Pak Sf Und Art Sf Lage der H.Gruppen im Osten- Stand 1.12.1943*, Panzer Ersatteilbesprechung am 3.1.1944, Generalstab des Heeres, January 2, 1944

Deliveries of Marders to the infantry divisions often occurred in batches to implement directives from Berlin. For example, most of the May and June 1943 deliveries of the Marder III Ausf H were used to help reconstruct infantry divisions that had been lost in Stalingrad. Likewise, most of the January and February 1944 deliveries were used to build up infantry divisions in France in the face of the anticipated Allied invasion.

In April 1943, the General Inspector of Panzer Troops, Heinz Guderian, held meetings to discuss the future of antitank defense. The obvious conclusion was that the antitank weapons of the infantry divisions were completely inadequate. Excessive numbers of trained troops, prime movers, and supplies were being wasted by being tied down to the light 3.7cm antitank gun platoons. The solution was to reduce the overall number of antitank guns per division by deleting the 3.7cm gun, but to increase the number of 7.5cm Pak 40s. As a result, a crash program was initiated with a goal of equipping each division with at least 12 7.5cm Pak 40 guns in the divisional Panzerjäger Abteilung. This was accomplished by July 1943, with most of the 7.5cm Pak 97/38s transferred to the West for use in the Atlantikwall. The next objective was to raise the average number of towed

A 7.5cm Marder III Ausf. M of Panzerjäger-Abteilung 61, 11.Panzer-Division, knocked out during fighting with the US 6th Armored Division on November 22, 1944 near St. Jean Rohrbach. This is from the post July-1943 production series when the exhaust pipe was routed externally on the right side of the hull.

7.5cm Pak 40s in the infantry divisions to 27 to permit each regimental Panzerjäger company to have a Zug of three or four 7.5cm Pak 40 guns. This objective was reached in December 1943.

A typical example of the changing antitank firepower on the Ostfront can be seen in a strength report from the 17.Armee. In June 1943, it had ten divisions under its command with 140 5cm Pak 38s (62 percent) and 85 heavy antitank guns (38 percent), averaging about 22 medium/heavy antitank guns per division. By November 1943, it had been reduced to three infantry divisions when it defended the Kuban bridgehead. Although the divisional arsenals had switched away from light antitank guns in favor of more medium and heavy antitank guns, the overall strength was poor with only 51 towed and self-propelled guns in the three divisions, averaging only 17 medium/heavy antitank guns per division. These included 13 5cm Pak 38s, nine 7.5cm Pak 97/38s, 16 7.5cm Pak 40s, and 13 Marder 7.5cm Pak Sfls.

The heyday of the Marder was 1943, due to the rapid increase in production. The Panzerjäger constituted near a fifth of total German Panzer and AFV production in 1942, as can be seen on the accompanying chart.

Comparative German AFV production by type, 1941–44

	Panzer	(%)	Sturmgeschütz	(%)	Panzerjäger	(%)	Total
1941	3,256	85.7	540	14.2	0	0	3,796
1942	4,278	69.5	748	12.1	1,123	18.2	6,149
1943	5,966	55.5	3,406	31.6	1,375	12.7	10,747
1944	9,161	50.1	8,682	47.4	441	2.4	18,284

As was the case with most armored vehicles, the vast bulk of Marder strength was deployed on the Ostfront in 1942 and 1943. Modest numbers of Marders were deployed to North Africa, the Balkans, and Italy in 1943. The chart here shows that in the final months of 1943, about 72 percent of Marder strength was on the Ostfront. This changed in 1944 as more resources were shifted to the West in anticipation of the Allied invasion of France.

Comparative Marder strength: Ost vs other fronts, 1943

	31 Oct			30 Nov			31 Dec		
	Ost	Other	**Total**	Ost	Other	**Total**	Ost	Other	**Total**
Marder II 7.62cm	27	5	**32**	12	11	**23**	11	11	**22**
Marder III 7.62cm	46	26	**72**	49	31	**80**	38	33	**71**
Marder I 7.5cm	41	80	**121**	40	81	**121**	37	94	**131**
Marder II 7.5cm	227	28	**255**	202	38	**240**	196	43	**239**
Marder III 7.5cm	427	116	**543**	378	128	**506**	408	98	**506**
Total	**768**	**255**	**1,023**	**681**	**289**	**970**	**690**	**279**	**969**

Source: Pak-Lage-Ost (Sf), Gen Qu GenInsGenPzTp, Jan 1944

At the time of the battle of Kursk in July 1943, there were 334 Marder Panzerjäger in units assigned to Operation *Zitadelle*, compared to 1,491 Panzers and 141 StuG IIIs, comprising about 15 percent of the armored combat vehicles. Of these, 96 served in Panzer divisions, 119 in Heer (army) and Waffen-SS Panzergrenadier divisions, 89 in infantry divisions, and 30 with PzJgAbt 561.

Panzerjäger at Kursk, July 1943

	HG Mitte	HG Süd	Total
PzSfl 1 (7.62cm)	4		**4**
PzSfl 2 (7.62cm)	6	39	**45**
Marder I (7.5cm)	15		**15**
Marder II (7.5cm)	94	61	**155**
Marder III (7.5cm)	95	20	**115**
Total	**214**	**120**	**334**

The Marder was the second most significant combat vehicle on the Ostfront through 1943 behind the Panzer, and more numerous than the Sturmgeschütz, averaging about a quarter of German armored strength that

The 7.5cm Pak 40/4 auf RSO was an attempt to create a simple and inexpensive Panzerjäger by mounting the 7.5cm Pak 40 on the chassis of the Raupenschlepper Ost prime mover. It was not well regarded due to its lack of armored protection, and only a trials batch of 60 were built including this example captured by the US Army in 1945.

year. This trend is evident on the accompanying chart. It's worth noting that the Sturmgeschütz began to take a lead on the Panzerjäger in the final month of 1943, a trend that would continue in 1944 as Marder production began to fade.

Panzer and AFV deployment on Ostfront, 1943

	May 31	Jun 30	Jul 31	Aug 31	Sep 30	Oct 20	Nov 20	Dec 31
Panzer	2,159	2,534	2,224	1,972	1,703	2,092	2,111	2,238
Pak Sfl*	766	1,022	1,054	1,093	1,119	1,425	1,435	1,453
StuG	855	994	956	924	1,047	1,165	1,273	1,507
Total	**3,780**	**4,550**	**4,234**	**3,989**	**3,869**	**4,682**	**4,819**	**5,198**

*Includes types other than Marder, such as 4.7cm and 8.8cm PzSfl

Like most German weapons on the Ostfront in 1943, there were continuing shortages of Marder Panzerjäger in 1943, despite the increased production rates. As a result, very few units reached their official authorized strength. In January 1944, Guderian, the General Inspector of Panzer Troops, conducted a survey of units on the Ostfront, comparing authorized strength versus actual strength. As is evident on the accompanying chart, Panzerjäger strength was only about 60 percent of authorized strength. This was worst in the Panzer divisions. Preference had been shown to the Panzer divisions in 1942, when there was a shortage of tanks with long 7.5cm guns. However, by 1943, the long-barreled versions of the PzKpfw IV were widely available, reducing the need for self-propelled heavy antitank guns. As a result, the preference for the supply of Panzerjäger was shifted to other units, especially the separate Heeres Panzerjäger Abteilungen. Infantry divisions still had low priority for self-propelled antitank guns, with only about a third of the infantry divisions on the Ostfront receiving a self-propelled Panzerjäger company.

Shortage of Pak Sfl on January 31, 1944

	No of Units	Requirement	Deployed	Shortage
Heeres PzJg Abteilungen	16	720	526	194
PzJg Abt in Panzer divisions	31	1,395	252	1,143
PzJg Abt in Panzergrenadier divisions	8	248	65	183
PzJg Ko. in Infanterie divisions	49	686	358	328
Total		**3,049**	**1,201**	**1,848**

Increased production of the 7.5cm Pak 40 and the associated 7.5cm Marder Pak Sfl in 1943 led to some field experiments with the infantry divisional Panzerjäger Kompanie and Abteilung. In some cases, the divisional antitank companies were incorporated into the infantry division's Füsilier Bataillon to create a *Schnell Bataillon* (Fast Battalion) to provide the division with a unit with better mobility and firepower.

The trend towards the end of 1943 was the creation of a "mixed" (gem: *gemischt*) Panzerjäger Abteilung. The innovation in this formation is that it substituted a Sturmgeschütz assault gun company for one of the antitank companies. This was widely approved, since most infantry commanders felt that the StuG III was a more versatile infantry support weapon than the Marder due to its full armored protection. This allowed it to be used alongside the infantry during close-combat assaults, a tactic that was very dangerous with the Marder due to the exposed crew.

Divisional Panzerjäger companies were still heavily dependent on towed 7.5cm Pak 40 anti-tank guns due to the shortage of Panzerjäger. This is a 7.5cm Pak 40 and its SdKfz. 11 half-track prime mover abandoned while on retreat in Belarus on June 27, 1944 during the Red Army's Operation *Bagration* summer offensive.

The mixed Panzerjäger Abteilung was authorized under the new Infanterie-Division 44 organization that began to appear in late 1943. This organization had a bewildering number of variations, so its organization can only be briefly summarized here. It usually had three companies and could typically include a StuG III company, a Marder company, and a company of towed 7.5cm Pak 40 guns. But these battalions sometimes substituted a 2cm Flak company for one of the antitank gun companies, and there was a trend in mid-1944 to substitute the low-cost 8.8cm Panzerschreck antitank rocket launchers for the 7.5cm Pak 40 in one company.

A good example of the varying approaches to self-propelled antitank weapons in the infantry division by 1944 can be seen in the accompanying chart showing the infantry divisions that saw combat in Normandy in June 1944. The Bodenständig divisions were second-class divisions used for coastal defense. They were typically equipped with the arthritic Marder I on the Lorraine Schlepper in their divisional Panzerjäger company and lacked

F

MARDER II PAK SFL 7.5cm PAK 40/2

1. Marder II, 11./Panzergrenadier-Regiment Hermann Göring.2, Italy, autumn 1943. This Luftwaffe Marder II was named *Raudi* (Rowdy) with the name on both sides of the superstructure front. It also had an odd cartoon dragon painted on the right side below the name. It was finished in RAL 7028 dark yellow, with large airbrushed blotches of RAL 8017 red brown.

2. Marder II, 2./Panzerjager-Abt.50, 9.Panzer-Division, Normandy, July 1944. The 9.Panzer-Division was scheduled to receive the Marder II in August 1942, finally completing delivery in January 1943. These old vehicles were supposed to be replaced in July 1944 with Jagdpanzer IV, but they did not arrive prior to the division's dispatch from southern France to Normandy. The camouflage scheme on this vehicle is the old dark grey RAL 7021 over which has been applied a loose pattern of airbrushed swatches of RAL 7028 dark yellow, RAL 6003 olive green and RAL 8017 red brown. The four digit tactical number was the result of a new policy implemented by the Gen. Ins.der.Pz.Tp. on April 24, 1944, codifying the numbering systems within the division. The first number was assigned to sub-units, for example "4" (Aufklärung Abteilung), "5" (Panzerjäger-Abteilung); "6" (Artillerie Regiment). The second number indicated the company, the third indicated the platoon, and the fourth number indicated the individual tank. The 9.Panzer-Division was one of the few if not the only Panzer division in Normandy to use this system in the summer of 1944.

2

newer weapons such as the 7.5cm Pak 40. The regular infantry divisions were in the new Type 1944 configuration with a Panzerjäger Abteilung (gem) benefiting from a company each of the Marder III and the StuG III.

Infantry division Panzerjäger units in Normandy, June 1944

Infantry divisions*	Marder I	Marder III	StuG
16.Lw			10
243.		14	10
326.		14	10
331.		14	10
346.		14	10
352.		14	10
353.		14	10
708.(b)	10		
709.(b)	10		
711.(b)	10		
716.(b)	10		
Total	**40**	**84**	**70**

**Lw: Luftwaffe, (b)= bodenständig*

Marder combat losses reached a peak in the summer of 1944 due to the Normandy fighting as well as the Red Army's devastating Operation *Bagration* offensive that crushed Heeresgruppe Mitte. The losses peaked in July 1944, as is evident in the accompanying chart.

A Marder III (7.5cm Pak 40) of Panzerjäger-Abteilung.10, 10.Panzergrenadier-Division hit by a large caliber high explosive round from a field gun of the Soviet 5th Artillery-Division while fighting around Ponyri Station on July 14, 1943 during the battle of Kursk.

Marder losses, December 1943–November 1944

Ost	**12/43 to 5/44**	**Jun**	**Jul**	**Aug**	**Sep**	**Oct**	**Nov**	**Total**
Pak Sf 7.5cm Pz II	96	2	49	7	7	2	6	**169**
Pak Sf. 7.5cm Pz38(t)	295	11	264	44	65	10	12	**701**
Pak Sf 7.5cm LrS	12	2	6		1			**21**
Pak Sf 7.62cm Pz II	16							**16**
Pak Sf 7.62cm Pz38(t)	29				2		2	**33**
West								
Pak Sf 7.5cm Pz II	2	5			6	2	1	**16**
Pak Sf. 7.5cm Pz38(t)	30	15	10	24	71		1	**151**
Pak Sf 7.5cm LrS	1	9	5		55			**70**
Pak Sf 7.62cm Pz II			10	24	17			**51**
Pak Sf 7.62cm Pz38(t)			5			1		**6**
Süd Ost								
Pak Sf 7.62cm Pz38(t)	3							**3**
Süd West								
Pak Sf 7.5cm Pz II		1						**1**
Pak Sf. 7.5cm Pz38(t)	23	30		3	8	3		**67**
Pak Sf 7.62cm Pz II		1						**1**
Pak Sf 7.62cm Pz.38(t)		17						**17**
Total	**507**	**93**	**349**	**102**	**232**	**18**	**22**	**1,323**

Source: *Monatsmeldungen, Anlage 4: Kraftfahrzeugen (Panzert)*, OKH, various months

MARDER'S REPLACEMENT

The creation of mixed Panzerjäger Abteilungen in late 1943 made it clear that the Sturmgeschütz was a superior alternative to the Marder as an infantry support weapon. Since the crew was entirely protected by armor, the StuG III could be used in close-combat tactics where the Marder would have been too vulnerable.

The main problem with replacing the Marder with the StuG III was that there was already a perennial shortage of StuG IIIs. This was exacerbated when the Alkett plant in Berlin-Borsigwalde, the main StuG III manufacturer, was hit by an RAF bombing raid on November 26, 1943. The HWA considered switching BMM from the production of the Marder to the StuG III, but discovered it did not have the capabilities to manufacture such a large vehicle. As a result, a program began to develop a "*Sturmgeschütz neuer Art*" that could be built at both BMM and Škoda in Plzeň (Pilsen). The design was influenced by the Romanian Maresal assault gun, and the new vehicle was ready for production in April 1944. Although originally called a Sturmgeschütz, Guderian, as head of the General Inspectorate for

A SdKfz 251/22 7.5cm Pak 40 from the 11.Panzer-Division captured by the US Army at the end of the war. This is a conversion by the WUMAG plant, not a field conversion.

Panzer Troops, insisted that it be designated as a Jagdpanzer instead. While this may seem like a minor semantic difference, the Jagdpanzer, like the Panzerjäger, was subordinated to the Panzer force, while the Sturmgeschütz was the responsibility of the artillery branch. As a result, the new vehicle was designated as the Jagdpanzer 38. It is better known today by its unofficial nickname of Hetzer.

With the Jagdpanzer 38 entering production in May, manufacture of the Marder III Ausf M at the BMM plant was brought to a close, the final vehicles being completed in May 1944. As can be seen from the accompanying chart, the end of Marder production led to a very sharp decline in the number deployed in the various combat theaters due to battlefield attrition, with only 438 by the end of 1944 compared to 1,848 in January 1944.

Marder deployment, December 30, 1944

Army group	Theater	7.5cm M II	7.5cm M III	7.62cm M II	7.62cm M III
HG Süd	Ost	14	30		
HG A	Ost	20	162	3	9
HG Mitte	Ost	29	37	2	6
HG Nord	Ost	8	10		3
Danemark	West	8	5		
HG H	West	1	2		3
HG B	West		15		1
HG G	West	7	4		
HG C	Süd West	1	49		
HG F	Süd Ost	9			
Total*		**97**	**314**	**5**	**22**

*8 Marder I in Heeresgruppe G
Source: *Lage der gepanzerten Kraftfahrzeuge sowie Beutepanzer-Lage zum 30. Dez 1944*, Generalinspekteur der Panzertruppen, January 22, 1945

SdKfz 251/22

In October 1944, the General Inspectorate for Panzer Troops revived the Marder concept by adding the 7.5cm Pak 40 on different chassis, the SdKfz 251 medium armored half-tracks and SdKfz 234 armored cars. Both types were already being produced with a 7.5cm KwK L/24 gun. However, this short-barrel gun was not very effective in the antitank role. At first, there was some skepticism that such a powerful weapon as the Pak 40 could be accommodated on such light vehicles due to its recoil forces. An experimental mounting of the 7.5cm KwK L.48 from the PzKpfw IV tank was also considered but ultimately rejected. Neither of these were envisioned as a replacement for the Marder series, since they were not intended for the infantry Panzerjäger companies, but rather for specialized roles in the Panzergrenadier and *Aufklärung* (reconnaissance) units.

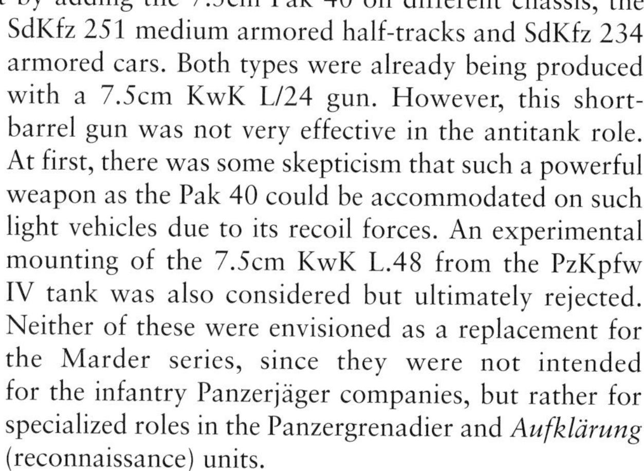

To test the concept, a 7.5cm Pak 40 was mounted into an unmodified SdKfz 251 Ausf D troop carrier by attaching the existing gun carriage, minus the wheel

The conversion of the SdKfz 251 to carry the 7.5cm Pak 40 required the addition of a substantial steel frame attached to the vehicle frame as seen in this interior view.

assembly and trails, on a special platform fitted in the hull behind the driver's compartment. The platform consisted of a welded table attached directly to the vehicle frame. Two ready racks for ammunition containing ten rounds were positioned on the right side of the gun mount for the loader, while additional ammunition could be carried elsewhere in the fighting compartment in the usual transport containers. One of the only changes needed to the gun was to cut away small sections of the splinter shield to provide better traverse within the confines of the superstructure. The conversion proved to be straightforward. In a November 27, 1944 meeting with armaments minister Speer, Hitler enthusiastically supported the idea. He recommended that all SdKfz 251/9 produced in November be withheld from deployment so that they could be converted from the short 7.5cm KwK L/24 to the much more powerful Pak 40. Aside from new production vehicles, Hitler also instructed that conversion kits be prepared so that field workshops could convert half-tracks to the new SdKfz 251/22 configuration. Hitler was so enamored of the new vehicle that at a December 5, 1944 display of new weapons, he labeled the SdKfz 251/22 as "one of the best technical solutions in this war."

A number of conversions from the SdKfz 251/9 to SdKfz 251/22 were done in the field using conversion kits. Judging from the disparity in the painted camouflage on the 7.5cm Pak 40 versus the SdKfz 251 hull, this may have been one such conversion. It was captured by the US Army in 1945.

Production of new SdKfz 251/22s was assigned to WUMAG (*Waggon und Maschinenbau AG*) in Görlitz. The first 40 were completed in December 1944 and a further 41 in January 1945. About 15 were completed in February 1945, but the plant ceased production due to the advance of the Red Army. Besides the new production vehicles, the first 68 conversion kits were completed in early December 1944 to convert the SdKfz 251/9 into the SdKfz 251/22 configuration. A total of about a hundred conversion sets were completed.

There was no formal deployment scheme for the SdKfz 251/22 until the release of the Panzer-Division 45 table of organization issued in March 1945. Under this plan, the SdKfz 251/22 was intended to be deployed as a Zug of three vehicles in the headquarters of Panzerjäger Abteilungen. Most Panzer units that received the SdKfz 251/22 presumably deployed the vehicles to fill gaps in their Panzergrenadier regiments.

SdKfz 234/4

The development of an armored car mounting for the 7.5cm Pak 40 paralleled the half-track version. The program began in October 1944 and by early the following month Büssing-NAG had completed the design. The process was accelerated by the fact that work had already been undertaken to mount the failed 7.5cm Kanone 51 in the SdKfz 234. The mounting was intended primarily to provide greater firepower to the Panzer-Aufklärung Abteilungen in Panzer divisions. Production began in December 1944 but proceeded at a very slow rate, with only about 90 completed through April 1945. There was no organized deployment plan, the vehicles being issued as replacements.

A SdKfz 234/4 7.5cm Pak, probably from the Panzer-Aufklärungs-Abteilung FHH of the Feldherrnhalle Korps, near the Czech town of Lázně Kynžvart on May 9, 1945 while elements of the unit were surrendering to the US Army.

Marder in cobelligerent service

The Wehrmacht was perennially short of tank destroyers and so was very frugal in reinforcing the cobelligerent armies on the Ostfront. The only known case of a program authorized by Berlin was the sale of 18 Marder IIIs to the Slovak Army in May 1944. These saw no combat against the Red Army but were turned against the Wehrmacht in September 1944 during the Slovak national uprising.

Although there were few formal sales, small numbers of vehicles were sometimes transferred out of local theater stocks. For example, in early 1943, the Hungarian Army received five Marder IIs to make up for losses in the Stalingrad campaign. They were used to create the 1st Separate Tank Destroyer Company that fought on the Don River front in 1943. In the summer of 1944, the Hungarian 1st Cavalry Division was crushed in the aftermath of the Soviet *Bagration* offensive, losing nearly all its armored vehicles. The Wehrmacht transferred a battery of Marder IIIs to the division when it served in the fighting around Warsaw in August 1944.

A Marder II of the Hungarian 1st Separate Tank Destroyer Company during operations along the river Don in January 1943. These were transferred from German theater stocks and retained their German markings.

MARDER COMBAT LESSONS

The Marder tank destroyer was an emergency solution to the problem of the growing weight of antitank guns. This problem was not unique to the Wehrmacht and was encountered by the British with the 17-pdr and by the US with the 3in. antitank gun. Both Britain and the United States responded by placing a portion of their heavy antitank guns on tank chassis. The majority of Allied tank destroyers were based on medium tank chassis, notably the M10 Gun Motor Carriage, a variant of the M4 Sherman tank. While the armored protection on the M10 was not as good as on a conventional tank, it was considerably better than on the Marder. Furthermore, the chassis was large enough to accommodate a greater amount of ammunition.

Germany put their 7.62cm and 7.5cm heavy antitank guns on obsolete light tank chassis due to overcommitment of existing medium tank production to more important types of armored vehicles. As a result, the German Panzerjäger chassis were too light to support comprehensive armored protection. While the Marder was a more effective weapon than towed antitank guns, it was still an imperfect solution compared to other types of armored vehicles.

A detailed analysis of the combat effectiveness of the Marder series is difficult due to the lack of comprehensive statistical data. Although the General Inspectorate for Panzer Troops did collect and disseminate data on both the Panzer and Sturmgeschütz, the Panzerjäger was frequently ignored. For example, the *Panzerlage* (tank status) for the battle of Kursk provides considerable detail on Panzer and Sturmgeschütz strength and losses during the battle, but ignores the Panzerjäger force. This is probably because a large portion of the Panzerjäger force was dispersed in small company-sized formations in the infantry divisions, outside the Panzer force's chain of reporting. Likewise, tank-kill claims collected by the OKH usually omit Panzerjäger units or lumps them in with Sturmgeschütz or antitank guns.

The Slovak Army purchased 18 Marder III Ausf. H that arrived in June 1944. Of these, 16 served with the Pluk útočnej vozby (Assault Vehicle Regiment) during the Slovak uprising against the Germans including this one that was knocked out during the fighting in September 1944.

One of the few Panzer Aces associated with the Marder was Unteroffizier Helmut Kohlke who commanded a Marder II named *Kohlenklau* (coal bandit) of 3./Panzerjäger Abt. 561 on the Ostfront in 1943. His barrel is decorated with 19 kill rings, but the majority of these were claimed when he served on a 5cm Pak 38 towed anti-tank gun.

Other sources can provide some hints. In 2005, historian Ron Klages published a list of "Panzer aces" on the Axis History Forum based on awards to Knight's Cross winners and other similar award lists. Although there were numerous addendums over the years, the basic list provides a very illuminating insight into German armored vehicle-kill claims since Knight's Crosses were often awarded to German soldiers for such accomplishments. Of more than 150 "Panzer aces," 30 were tank crewmen, of which 22 were Tiger crew. The largest portion were StuG III crew, numbering around 110. About a half-dozen were crew for various types of Jagdpanzer, such as the Elefant and Nashorn, and five were towed antitank guns. There were no Marder crews listed.

G

MARDER III AUSF. M

1. Marder III Ausf. M, 1./ Panzerjäger-Abteilung 305, 305.Infanterie-Division, Gustav Line, Italy, May 1944. This Marder III Ausf. M was finished in overall RAL 7028 dark yellow with large clouds of RAL 8017 red brown thinly airbrushed over the base coat. The 1.Kompanie carried the divisional insignia of a pine tree on the right side of the superstructure front as seen here, along with the vehicle number, 14 in black. One the other side was the German tactical map symbol for a Panzerjäger unit in black. Each of the unit vehicles had a name such as Sultana, Luchs, etc.

2. Marder III Ausf. M, 1./ Panzerjäger-Abteilung 243, 243.Infanterie-Division, Normandy, June 1944. This Marder III Ausf. M is finished in the usual scheme consisting of a base color of RAL 7028 dark yellow, with airbrushed splotches of RAL 6003 olive green and RAL 8017 red brown. The markings on the superstructure side include the tactical number 112 in black with white trim and the *Balkenkreuz*.

1
14
14
Sultana
2
112

There have been some suggestions that the Panzerjäger crews were simply missed off the list. For example, Unteroffizier Helmut Kohlke of Panzerjäger-Abteilung 561 was awarded the Iron Cross 1st and 2nd Class and the German Cross in Gold. However, the source of many of these awards appears to have been for tank kills claimed while on the crew of a 5cm Pak 38, and only a portion of his roughly 20 kill claims were while he served in a Marder II.

Regardless of the precise number of Panzerjäger crewmen who received exceptional awards, the performance of the Panzerjäger was lackluster compared to the Sturmgeschütz. It seems likely that this was due to the vulnerability of the crew on the Marder tank destroyers rather than problems with the vehicle's firepower. The chance of becoming a "Panzer ace" decreased in proportion to the probability of becoming a combat casualty. Since Panzerjäger crew were so vulnerable, their chance of surviving to become a "Panzer ace" were slim. In contrast, the Sturmgeschütz crew enjoyed complete armored cover from the most widespread battlefield threats such as small-arms fire, antitank rifles, and artillery fragments.

Marder strength and losses, 1942–45

Strength	**1942**	**1943**	**1944**	**1945**
Jan		1,124	1,306	581
Feb		1,222	1,314	529
Mar		1,063	1,361	
Apr		889	1,353	
May	128	840	1,205	
Jun	270	812	1,241	
Jul	306	971	1,160	
Aug	480	1,110	851	
Sep	600	1,105	774	
Oct	680	1,102	608	
Nov	850	1,170	596	
Dec	980	1,277	477	
Losses	**1942**	**1943**	**1944**	**1945**
Jan		5	70	48
Feb		220	58	52
Mar		119	22	
Apr		82	156	
May		98	33	
Jun		1	75	
Jul	15	76	306	
Aug	25	75	64	
Sep	35	25	166	
Oct	24	46	12	
Nov	23	19	19	
Dec	5	67		
Total	**127**	**833**	**981**	**100**

Source: GenMaj Hermann Burkhardt, *Tank Strength and Loss Statistics*, Appendix 3, US Army Foreign Military Studies P-059, 1947.

FURTHER READING

The technical aspects of the Marder Panzerjäger have been amply detailed in various monographs in the Nuts & Bolts series as well as Tom Jentz's essential Panzer Tracts series. The combat history of the vehicles has not been as well documented. Besides these published accounts, the author made extensive use of primary sources, including the records of the General Inspectorate for Panzer Troops found in record group RH 10 at the Bundesarchiv and record group RG-252, T-78 at the US National Archives and Records Administration in College Park, Maryland.

Andorfer, Volker, et al., *Marder III Panzerjäger 38(t) für 7.62cm Pak 36*, Nuts & Bolts, Neumünster (2009)

Andorfer, Volker, et al., *Marder III Panzerjäger 38(t) für 7.5cm Pak 40/3 Ausführung H*, Nuts & Bolts, Neumünster (2004)

Andorfer, Volker, et al., *Marder III Panzerjäger 38(t) für 7.5cm Pak 40/3 Ausführung M*, Nuts & Bolts, Neumünster (2004)

Baschin, J., *PzKpfw II Ausf. D/E and Variants*, Nuts & Bolts, Neumünster (2013)

Baschin, J. & Block, M., *Marder II Panzerjäger II für 7.5cm Pak 40/2*, Nuts & Bolts, Neumünster (2013)

Charpentier, Loïc, *L'artillerie antichar allemande durant la seconde guerre mondiale*, Caraktère, Aix-en-Provence (2022)

Degtev, Dmitriy & Zubov, D., *Divizionaya pushka F-22*, Yauza, Moscow (2022)

Francev, V. & Kliment, C., *Marder III & Grille*, MBI, Praha (1999)

Guglielmi, Daniele & Pieri, Mario, *Italienfeldzug: German Tanks and Vehicles 1943–45*, Vol 2, Ammo of Mig, Estella (2020)

Jentz, Thomad & Doyle, Hilary, *Panzerjaeger 7.62cm FK (r) auf gp.Sfl. to Marder 38T*, Panzer Tracts, Boyds (2005)

INDEX